Vauxhall Branch Libra

D1062641

Signs in My World

Signs at the Store

By Mary Hill

Vauxhall Branch Library

Children's Press®
A Division of Scholastic Inc.
New York / Toronto / London / Auckland / Sydney
Mexico City / New Delhi / Hong Kong
Danbury, Connecticut

Thanks to Acme Markets in Media, PA

Photo Credits: Cover and all photos by Maura B. McConnell
Contributing Editor: Jennifer Silate
Book Design: Erica Clendening and Michelle Innes

Library of Congress Cataloging-in-Publication Data

Hill, Mary, 1977–
    Signs at the store / by Mary Hill.
    p. cm. — (Signs in my world)
    Includes index.
    Summary: On a trip to the grocery store with her father, Carly notices
    the various signs that help them, including those that show where to
    find certain items, what they cost, and which checkout line is open.
    ISBN 0-516-24271-7 (lib. bdg.) — ISBN 0-516-24363-2 (pbk.)
    1. Stores, Retail—Juvenile literature. 2. Shopping—Juvenile
    literature. 3. Signs and signboards—Juvenile literature. [1. Stores,
    Retail. 2. Grocery shopping. 3. Signs and signboards.] I. Title. II.
    Series.

    HF5429 .H523 2003
    641.3'1—dc21

                                                        2002006942

Copyright © 2003 by Rosen Book Works, Inc.
All rights reserved. Published simultaneously in Canada.
Printed in the United States of America.
1 2 3 4 5 6 7 8 9 10 R 12 11 10 09 08 07 06 05 04 03

Contents

My name is Carly.

Dad and I are going to the **grocery store**.

The store has many **signs**.

The signs tell us different things.

This sign shows how much the bread costs.

There is another sign.

It says, "**Deli**."

The deli has many kinds of meat.

There is a sign for each kind of meat.

Dad wants some turkey.

11

The signs above us tell what foods are kept in each row.

CAN VEGETABLES
CAN FRUIT
SOUP
GRAVY
PORK & BEAN

Dad wants sugar.

Here is a sign with "Sugar" written on it.

That means that we will find sugar in this row.

4

SUGAR
FLOUR
CAKE MIX
COOKING OIL
SPICES

15

Here is the sugar.

We have everything
we need.

Now, we must pay for our food.

There is a sign that says, "Open."

We will pay here.

OPEN OPEN

19

Dad pays the **cashier** for our food.

We are finished **shopping**.

21

New Words

cashier (**ka**-shihr) someone who takes in money in a store

deli (**deh**-lee) a place where one can buy meat and cheese

grocery store (**groh**-sur-ee **stor**) a store that sells food

shopping (**shop**-ing) going to stores to buy things

signs (**sinez**) public notices that give information

To Find Out More

Books
I Read Signs
by Tana Hoban
Greenwillow

Mama & Papa Have a Store
by Amelia Lau Carling
Penguin Putnam

Math at the Store
by William Amato
Scholastic Library Publishing

Index

About the Author
Mary Hill writes and edits children's books.

Reading Consultants
Kris Flynn, Coordinator, Small School District Literacy, The San Diego County
Office of Education

Shelly Forys, Certified Reading Recovery Specialist, W.J. Zahnow Elementary
School, Waterloo, IL

Sue McAdams, Former President of the North Texas Reading Council of the
IRA, and Early Literacy Consultant, Dallas, TX